This Travel Book belongs

to ....

Fun Travel Books Kids ©

Hi, my name is Tom Tomato and I'm a very special cherry tomato! Why? Because I'm a traveler! And I'm here to be your friend during this trip to

Barcelona!

Did you know...?

- Barcelona is the capital and largest city of the autonomous community of Catalunya.
- The "Futbol Club Barcelona" is one of the strongest team in the world. It's known as "Blaugrana" due to the colors of the sport uniform.
- The movie "Snowflake, the White Gorilla" was set in Barcelona. The film depicts the fictional childhood of the white gorilla Snowflake who lived in the City Zoo.
- The "Sagrada Familia" Basilica, designed by Gaudì, has been under construction since 1882!

THAT'S ME!

Tell me something about you...

My trip

From day: _____

To day: _____

With: _____

Transportation:

_____

Tell me about your trip

My journey

_____

_____

_____

_____

_____

My accommodation

This is the map of Barcelona. Giradabo ferris is the symbol of the Tibidabo Park.

Welcome to Barcelona

Some of the most beautiful monuments are the Cathedral of the Holy Cross and Saint Eulalia, The Arc de Triomf and obviously Gaudi's masterpieces: Park Güell, Casa Batlò, La Pedrera and the Sagrada Família Basilica.

DISTANCE TABLE

How far is Barcelona from...

City	Distance
Amsterdam	1.240 Km
Rome	861 Km
Lisbon	1.008 Km
London	1.140 Km
Berlin	1.501 Km
Madrid	506 Km
New York	6.174 Km
Los Angeles	9.667 Km
Moscow	3.014 Km
Tokyo	10.432 Km
Sidney	17.205 Km
My Home:	.... Km

- The official language in Barcelona is Catalan not Spanish.
- Tibidabo Amusement Park is the oldest amusement park of Spain. It's located on a hill called "the Magic Mountain"
- The name "Barcelona" comes from the ancient Iberian "Barkeno".

Gaudi

Antoni Gaudi i Cornet was an architect known as the greatest exponent of Catalan Modernism. Many of his masterpieces in Barcelona are included in UNESCO World Heritage. His burial is in the Sagrada Família.

Picasso

Pablo Ruiz Picasso was a painter and sculptor. Born in Malaga he demonstrated an extraordinary artistic talent already in his early years. He moved to Barcelona with his parents where he studied. Many of his artworks are displayed at the Picasso Museum.

Montserrat Caballé

María de Montserrat Caballé was an operatic soprano born in Barcelona. She became popular to non-classical music audiences when she recorded a duet with Freddie Mercury ("Barcelona, the official theme song for the 1992 Olympic Games).

Casa Batlò and Casa Milà (known as "La Pedrera") are two Gaudi's masterpieces. The first one has a roof arched and likened to the back of a dragon, the second one is grey with warrior-shaped statues on the roof.

La Barceloneta is known for its sandy beach and its many restaurants and nightclubs along the boardwalk. It made an appearance in the book "Don Quixote".

La Rambla is a tree-lined pedestrian street, plenty of cafes and souvenir kiosks. The Spanish poet Federico Garcia Lorca once said that La Rambla was "the only street in the world which I wish would never end."

Montjuïc translates to "Jewish Mountain" due to the remains of a medieval Jewish cemetery. You can go up to the "Mirador" with the cableway and at the top there are gardens, playgrounds, museums and sports facilities and the "Magic Fountain".

The Gothic Quarter (Barri Gòtic) is the historic center of the old city. Here you can see the Saint Cross and Saint Eulalia Cathedral, the Picasso Museum and the Museum of the History of Barcelona and taste the best churros ever.

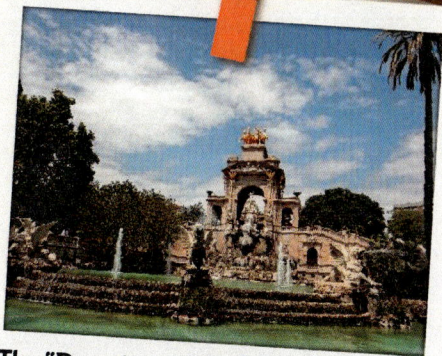

The "Parc de la Ciutadella" was built on the site of the old fortress. It includes the City Zoo (once home to the white gorilla Snowflake), the "Palau del Parlament de Catalunya", a small lake, museums, and a large fountain.

La Boqueria is a large public market and one of the city's foremost tourist landmarks. The market has a very diverse selection of goods and it's the perfect place to taste the original "Tapas".

....
....
....
....

DREAM CHECKLIST

Your dreams...

Write what you would like to visit/do/see during this trip

_____

_____

_____

_____

_____

_____

Dreaming Barcelona

Write or draw what you imagine...

SECRET CODE

A	B	C	D	E	F	G
🎩	🔭	📷	🍳	☸️	✈️	🛂

H	I	J	K	L	M	N
⛺	🕶️	🎸	🔥	🔪	🎈	🚂

O	P	Q	R	S	T	U
🛟	🎒	🏐	🚢	⌚	🛟	🌐

V	W	X	Y	Z
🕶️	🔥	🧭	🔑	🚌

Tom has a message for you
Crack the code!

Arc the Triomf

The "Arc de Triomf" is a triumphal arch built for the 1888 Barcelona World Fair. It doesn't celebrate a military victory but the artistic and scientific progress. Color it!

LEARN THE LANGUAGE

Nice to meet you

Good morning	Bon dia
My name is	El meu nom és
I am a child	Sóc un nen

Places

Museum	Museu
Restaurant	Restaurant
Train station	Estació de tren

Animals

Dog	Gos
Cat	Gat
Mouse	Ratolí

Something to eat

Ice cream	Gelat
Strawberry	Maduixa
Bread	Pa

While visiting

Painting	Obra d'art
Statue	Estàtua
Monument	Monument

Means of transportation

Airplane	Avió
Train	Tren
Car	Cotxe

Play with Catalan words

Connect the words with the pictures

Restaurant

Gat

Estàtua

Nens

Cotxe

Maduixa

Where is...?
Connect the picture with the right place

● Casa Milà (La Pedrera)

● Parc de la Ciutadella

● La Boqueria

● Parc Güell

MATCHING GAME

Would you play the Hangman Game?

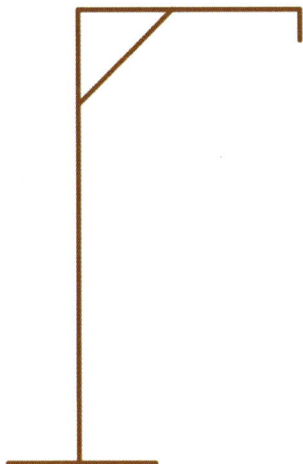

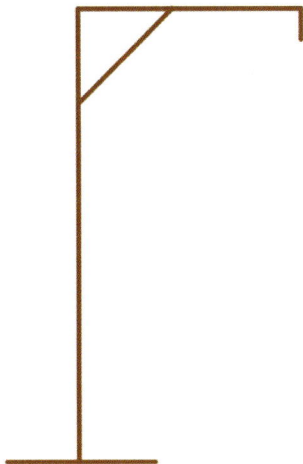

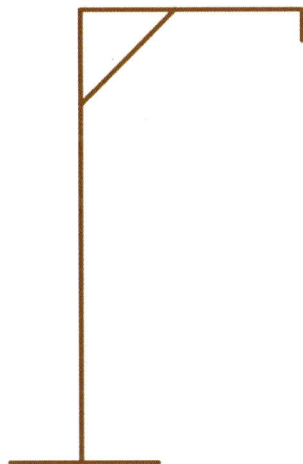

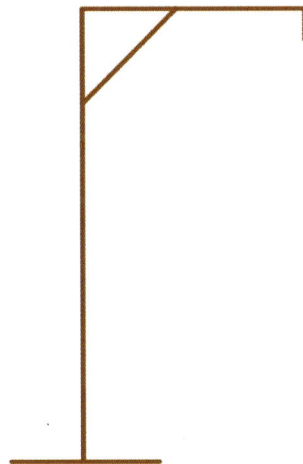

Find the missing piece!

Park Güell is a park designed by Gaudí, a fairy–tale place, with strange buildings, colored ceramic benches and mosaic salamanders. It was declared a World Heritage Site by UNESCO in the 1984.

COLOR

**Would you play
Tic Tac Toe?**

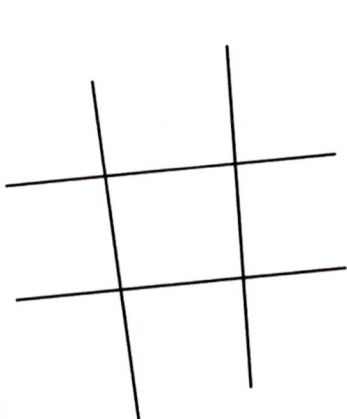

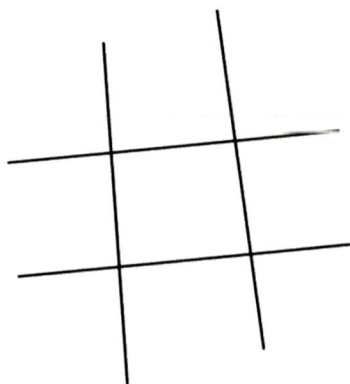

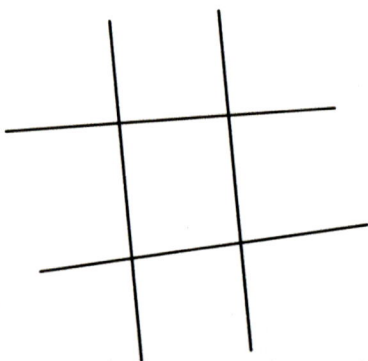

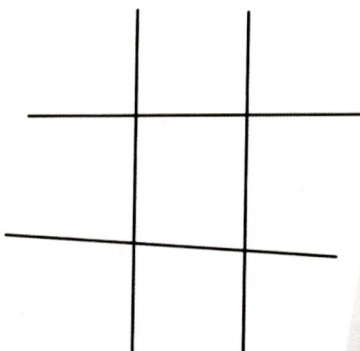

TIC TAC TOE

BECOME A PAINTER

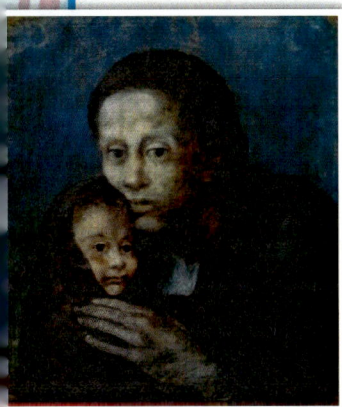

Draw like Picasso

The "Desemparats" is one of the Picasso's painting which represents a mother and a child. It's exhibited at the Picasso Museum. Try to draw them too!

Puzzle 1 (6×6)

6	3			1	
5				3	4
	5		2	6	
2		3		5	
3		5		4	
1		6	3	2	

Help Tom to solve the sudoku

Symbol Puzzle (4×4)

♣		♦	♥
	♦	♣	
♦		♠	♣
	♣		

Puzzle 2 (9×9)

2	6	7		5				
4				7	8	9		2
9		1		4	3		6	7
					5	7		4
						3		
8		5	4	3	7			
		8						
1	2		5					
	3			8		1		

SUDOKU

MAZE

Help Tom to go to the Sagrada Familia and his friend to get back his camera

WORD SEARCH

Find these words below

BOQUERIA   CATALONIA   EULALIA

FAMILIA   GAUDÌ   PEDRERA

PICASSO   RAMBLAS   TAPAS

T	A	P	G	J	A	O	T	Q	C
A	Y	I	K	A	S	N	B	A	A
P	P	L	L	S	U	O	Y	R	T
A	Z	E	A	I	Q	D	V	E	A
S	S	C	L	U	M	Z	Ì	R	L
L	I	H	E	P	Y	A	H	D	O
P	O	R	M	N	H	R	F	E	N
A	I	L	A	L	U	E	E	P	I
A	R	A	M	B	L	A	S	P	A
U	H	F	Y	M	E	Y	X	L	X

FIND THE PLACE

S_G__D_ F_____

Gaudi was buried there

E_L_L__

The Saint of the Cathedral

B__C_L_____

Barcelona's sea and beaches

M___J_ÏC

The place of the Magic Fountain

Use the clues to find the name of the tourist attractions

COLORING PAGE

Color Tom and tell him your day

FIND THE DIFFERENCES

Find the differences (5 in each image)

CROSS MATH

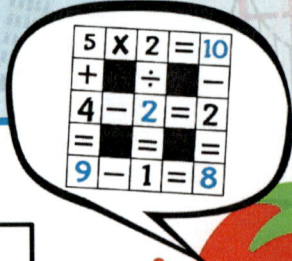

Math crossword puzzles

2	+		=	7
+	■	−	■	−
	−	4	=	
=	■	=	■	=
	−	1	=	6

Complete using math

5	x		=	10
+	■	÷	■	−
4	−	2	=	
=	■	=	■	=
	−		=	

DRAW & COLOR

1 2 3 4 5 6 7

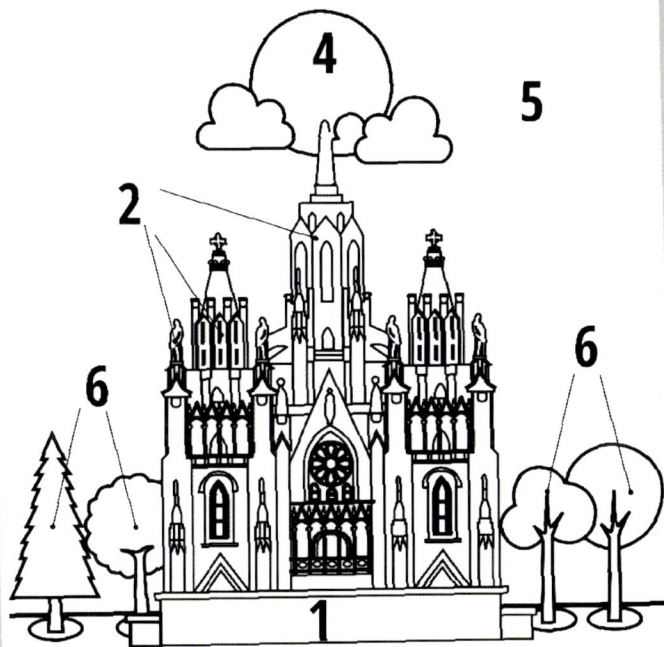

This is the Cathedral of the Holy Cross and Saint Eulalia. In the cloister there are 13 geese: they are the guardians of the sarcophagus of the Saint!

Each number corresponds to a color: paint the church!

GEOMETRIC DRAWING

Draw your day using the triangles

ONCE UPON A TIME

Create a fairy tale about Barcelona using these pictures

Once upon a time...

Things I've seen

Check what you have seen: did you like them?

☐ **La Pedrera**

☐ **Barceloneta**

☐ **Parc Güell**

☐ **Barri Gòtic**

☐ **La Rambla**

☐ **La Boqueria**

☐ **Sagrada Familia**

Draw or write what you loved the most!

z

What did you eat?

- [ ] **Tapas**

- [ ] **Esqueixada de bacallà**
  (salad with cod, tomatoes and olives)

- [ ] **Zarzuela**
  (fish soup)

- [ ] **Canelons a la Barcelonesa**
  (cannelloni stuffed with meat)

DESSERTS

- [ ] **Crema Catalana**
  (custard cream, with cinnamon and lemon)

- [ ] **Churros**
  (fritters served with hot chocolate)

★ **THE BEST CHOICE** ★
IN TOWN

My favorite dish is...

My best memories...

BY AIR MAIL
PAR AVION

NEW YORK N.Y.
MAY 10
7-PM
NO. 764538

PASSPORT

AIRMAIL

VISA

SOUVENIR

Stick your photos or souvenirs

My best memories!!

PICTURES

CUT OUT & PLAY

Cut the figures...

...and create your story

Fun Travel Books Kids ©

February 2020

funtravelbookskids@gmail.com

The adventures of Tom Tomato continue here

amazon.com

amazon.co.uk

Made in United States
North Haven, CT
02 June 2024